Wow!
JESUS

To Ellis, Esmé, Zeb, Zac, and Flissy
May you always seize the chance to be creative explorers
and know how much the ultimate Creator loves you.

Text copyright © 2023 Martha Shrimpton
Illustrations by Sarah Nolloth
This edition copyright © 2023 Lion Hudson IP Limited

Published by
Candle Books
www.lionhudson.com
Part of the SPCK Group
SPCK, 36 Causton Street, London, SW1P 4ST

ISBN 978 1 78128 425 4

First edition 2023

Acknowledgments
Designed by Karen Hood

A catalogue record for this book is available
from the British Library

Produced on paper from sustainable sources
Printed and bound in China, August 2023, LH54

Wow!
JESUS

Creatively explore stories in the Bible

MARTHA SHRIMPTON

ILLUSTRATED BY SARAH NOLLOTH

CANDLE
BOOKS

The Wow! Series

Connect creatively with your maker, your family, and your community with this series of books exploring stories and themes found in the Bible.

Wow! Hello creative explorer! I am so glad that you have joined me on this mission to unpack the epic stories about Jesus. What an exciting journey there is ahead! So, grab the rest of your creative team (friends and family) because we are about to dive into these stories by *playing*, *celebrating*, and *creating*. Let's go!

Pray || Pause || Play || Create || Celebrate || Communicate

PRAY
Wow! Hello God... Opportunities to pray in a creative way, by yourself or with others.

PAUSE
Wow! Time to pause... Take some time out to reflect on a part of the story, and how it fits with your life now.

PLAY
Wow! What a show... Ideas to get you on your feet and having a bit of fun exploring the story.

CREATE
Wow! Let's create! Fun crafts and creations that help you to explore some of the story's themes.

CELEBRATE
Wow! That's cool! Rejoice and celebrate together as you discover things that amaze you about God in each story.

COMMUNICATE
Wow! Can we chat? A chance to chat and connect with each other, using parts of the story as conversation starters.

TOP TIP!
At the start of each chapter, you will spot a passage reference to find in your Bible. This will lead you to the story we will be exploring together! So, why not read the story in your Bible before you start your creative journey?

To find more creative resources, including storytelling videos of each story by Martha, and creative ways of exploring Bible stories with your family and community, visit the Nimbus Collective website at www.nimbuscollective.org

Nimbus Collective is an organization founded by Martha Shrimpton. It is aimed at helping you to connect in a creative way with yourself, your community, and God.

Contents

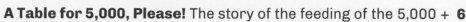
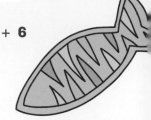
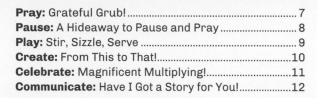

A Table for 5,000, Please!

The story of the feeding of the 5,000+

MATTHEW 14:13–21

There was a man called Jesus who *everyone* had been talking about!

News travels fast when someone is doing incredible things to help people and telling amazing stories that blow people's minds!

As you can imagine, things had been pretty busy for Jesus and his mates, so they'd gone to find some peace and quiet. But guess what? The crowd followed him!

Not just a small crowd, but a huge crowd of 5,000 people – and more. They stayed for a long time, listening, watching, and learning from Jesus. As the sun started to set, their stomachs began to rumble.

One of Jesus' mates brought a boy to him with a basket of two fish and five pieces of bread. He hoped that Jesus could use them, which of course he did!

Jesus thanked God for the food and started handing it out. Everyone got a chunk of bread and a nice piece of fish, with food to spare. This dinner stretched further than the turkey after Christmas day!

Not bad for a tiny packed lunch!

Wow! What a story! What a miracle!

WANT TO READ MORE?
Why not dive into the story by reading it in your Bible in **MATTHEW 14:13–21**?

OR you could start your creative adventure exploring this amazing story about Jesus right away!

GRATEFUL GRUB!

"Only five loaves and two fish!"

"It would cost us so much money to feed ALL these people!"

"Send them away to sort themselves out for the night!"

WOW! Everyone in this situation seemed to see the negative: how there wasn't enough food or money, and how there were just too many people!

Jesus, however, saw things differently. He saw the small amount of food as being just right and said THANK YOU to God for it – and it multiplied to a WAY bigger amount than before!

Sometimes, we can see things a little negatively. But noticing what we have and saying THANK YOU to God for what he has given us is really important! It changes the way we view things. God loves it when we are grateful, and he blesses us with more than we could ever imagine.

Let's get creative!

It's time to bring this story to life and get creative with our own FISH and BREAD!

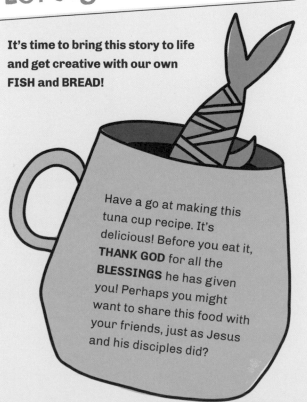

Have a go at making this tuna cup recipe. It's delicious! Before you eat it, **THANK GOD** for all the **BLESSINGS** he has given you! Perhaps you might want to share this food with your friends, just as Jesus and his disciples did?

TUNA CUP (MAKES 6)

YOU WILL NEED:

a muffin tin	1 tablespoon
spray oil	mayonnaise
1 tin of tuna	6 medium bread slices
60g (½ cup) frozen peas	grated cheese
and sweetcorn	

STEP 1 Preheat the oven to 190°C or gas mark 5.

STEP 2 Spray a little oil in six sections of the muffin tin. Flatten a slice of bread into each to make a bread "cup" with the crusts poking out of the top. Spray lightly with oil and bake for 10–15 mins.

STEP 3 In a bowl, mix the tuna, mayonnaise, peas, and sweetcorn.

STEP 4 Remove the bread cups and fill with the tuna mix. Sprinkle a little cheese on the top of each.

STEP 5 Bake for another 3-5 mins.

STEP 6 Remove from oven. GIVE THANKS TO GOD, tuck in, and ENJOY!

A HIDEAWAY TO PAUSE AND PRAY

Do you sometimes long to find a safe place where you can be alone for a while? A cosy place where you can hide away and just "be"? A "den" where you can imagine, dream, and chat with God?

Jesus was exactly the same! At the start and at the end of this story, we find Jesus trying to find a little spot where he could be alone – just him with God.

Let's get creative!

Make a HIDEAWAY of your own, where you can PAUSE and PRAY.

STEP 1 Grab some blankets and cushions.

STEP 2 Find a place (inside or outside) where you feel safe and peaceful.

STEP 3 Create your own cosy little den – get as creative as you like! You could use an umbrella as a roof or a blanket as a wall. You might want to make a little snack pack to take into your hideaway. Perhaps a hot chocolate could make it feel even more cosy!

STEP 4 Once you have created your little space, get into it. Take some time out with God, just to chat and listen.

STIR, SIZZLE, SERVE!

"AND WE ARE LIVE IN... 5... 4... 3... 2... 1!"

Imagine you are a world-class celebrity chef. You're on TV, in the cooking slot of one of the biggest morning chat-show programmes. The problem is you only have two ingredients to cook with! Two stinky fish and five little loaves of bread! What are you supposed to whip up with that?

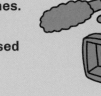

Let's act!

It's time for you to create a performance based on the story of "The Feeding of the 5,000" – with a twist!

Using the idea above, create a short scene where the TV chef is told they are **"live"** just as they are given the two ingredients to make something spectacular! How do they feel? What do they create? Is there a miracle that happens to help them turn the little they have into something amazing?

STEP 2

CREATE YOUR PLOT: Now that you have your character, think about how your scene will play out. Plan the opening, middle, and ending of your scene. Every good play has a "climax moment" where something goes wrong that the characters have to fix or overcome. What could the "climax moment" be in your scene?

TOP TIP: Create a "storyboard" (a plan of the structure of your story), setting out the order of events in your scene.

STEP 1

CREATE YOUR CHEF CHARACTER: Working alone or with other people, create your TV chef character. Do they have a funny voice or stand in a different way to you? Do they get flustered when things go wrong, or do they stay calm in a crisis?

TOP TIP: If you are working as part of a group, you might want to create more characters, such as a presenter character who will ask the chef questions, or a cooking assistant.

STEP 3

REHEARSE AND PERFORM: Now you have your character/s and scene structure, you can put the scene "on its feet" and start to create and rehearse your TV show. When you're ready, why not perform your scene to an audience?

TOP TIP: To make a really good performance, try to use fewer words and tell the story through the character's facial expressions and body language to create a great, entertaining piece of theatre!

Wow! Let's create!

FROM THIS TO THAT

The boy who gave his lunch to Jesus' disciples must have been amazed by what became of his little meal of fish and bread!

Stained-glass windows have colourful pieces of glass that join together to make a picture. When the light hits the glass, often the colours are projected onto the floor or walls, creating an even bigger picture than the one you can see in the window!

The windows are beautiful already, but the colourful shadows when the sun hits the stained glass make them even better.

You might need an adult to help with some of these steps.

Let's get creative!

Create your own stained-glass fish to put into a window.

When the light hits it, remember the amazement of the boy in this story when his fish were used in an incredible way!

YOU WILL NEED:

card
pens
clear plastic (such as
    an old plastic sleeve,
    or a wrapper)
tissue paper
PVA glue

STEP 1 Draw an outline of a fish on card big enough to fill your window and cut it out. Cut out the centre to create a fish shape border.

STEP 2 Attach clear plastic to the middle of the fish shape.

STEP 3 Gather multiple different colours of tissue paper and cut into several little shapes.

STEP 4 Using PVA glue, cover the clear plastic part of your fish with tissue-paper shapes to make a multicoloured collage.

STEP 5 When dry, hang the fish in a window where sun will shine through it. Enjoy the shapes and colours that are made by the light!

AHHH!

WOW!

MAGNIFICENT MULTIPLYING!

Isn't it amazing how the disciples handed out the food and it never ran out? It kept on multiplying – even to the point where there were more baskets of food at the end than to start with!

Jesus already knew how he was going to use this food, which was barely enough for a few let alone 5,000 men PLUS women and children! He knew he was going to perform a miracle, something amazing and incredible to show everyone just how much he cared!

How do you think people felt when they saw this happening? Astounded? Surprised? Overjoyed? Disbelieving?

Let's get creative!

Why not think about this as you watch something increase before your very eyes too?

YOU WILL NEED:

a pan with a lid
3 tablespoons oil
40g (⅓ cup) popcorn kernels

Wow! Look at the popcorn!

STEP 1 Ask an adult to help you heat the oil in the pan on a medium heat.

STEP 2 Add 3–4 popcorn kernels to the pan. Cover and listen for the "pop" of the corn.

STEP 3 Once the corns have popped fully, add the rest of the popcorn kernels to the pan. When you hear each pop of the popcorn, imagine the amazement, surprise, and celebration of the crowd as they watched the food being multiplied.

STEP 4 Once the popping stops, give the pan a gentle shake and lift the lid.

A little really has turned into a lot! This is probably more than you could ever eat by yourself! Imagine how astonished the crowd were when Jesus fed them all. They must have had such a celebration!

Wow! Can we chat?

HAVE I GOT A STORY FOR YOU!

Imagine being in that crowd of 5,000 people and more. There were so many people! Before handing out the food, Jesus asked his disciples to get the crowd to sit in smaller groups.

Why do you think he did that? Maybe to make sharing out the food easier? Or perhaps it was to build community? To get people gathered with new friends and old, sharing stories and laughing as they ate delicious food together!

Eating food with friends outside can be so exciting and so much fun. Especially when you can tell stories and listen to others around you too!

Why don't you take the opportunity to do just that?

Let's get creative!

Pack a picnic, gather some friends, and find a spot to sit.

Share stories together about something you are thankful to God for. It could be something you notice in nature, a friend in your life, or the delicious food you're eating. Listening to others' stories and sharing our own can help us realize just how amazing God is!

So Many Fish!

The story of the fishermen casting their nets

LUKE 5:1–11

It was early days for Jesus in the epic journey ahead of him, but people had already started to hear about him and some of the amazing things he was doing.

A big group of people had come together to hear some of his wise words. Jesus decided to take a boat and row a little way out onto the lake so more people could see him.

As he headed out onto the water, he couldn't help noticing how worn out the fishermen looked. In fact, worn out was an understatement! After fishing all night, the fishermen had not even caught one fish so the bags under their eyes were the least of their worries!

After speaking to the crowd, Jesus offered the fishermen some help. "Why don't you drop the nets on the deep side of the boat?" he asked them.

The fishermen were a bit put off by Jesus' words. Didn't this Jesus think that they would have tried that?

The thing is, everyone knew Jesus had a way with words – when he said something, things usually happened. So the fishermen took the plunge and dropped their nets into the deep water.

All of a sudden, their nets got tight as if something was pulling them down even deeper. Hold up! Was this for real? The nets were full – bursting at the seams with big fish and little fish of all different kinds. They could not believe it!

Jesus spoke again. "Now, you guys, come with me! I'm going to teach you how to be fishermen of people!"

If the fishermen could witness more incredible things like this, there was no question about it. They dropped their nets and started their awesome adventure with Jesus!

Wow! What a story! What a miracle!

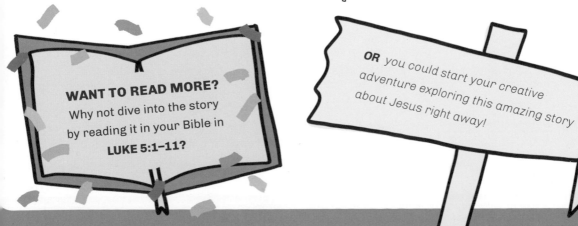

WANT TO READ MORE?
Why not dive into the story by reading it in your Bible in **LUKE 5:1–11?**

OR you could start your creative adventure exploring this amazing story about Jesus right away!

Wow! Hello God...

YOU ARE INVITED!

Isn't it amazing how Jesus calls and invites the disciples to be his friend, and to follow him on his journey? Not only that, he also says that he wants them to be fishermen of people! Fishermen of people? What does that mean?

Jesus is asking the disciples to tell other people about him and to invite them to be his friend. What's really cool is he is asking us to do that too!

One way we can do that is to pray for our friends and to TELL them we are praying for them!

Let's get creative!

Jesus invites us to be his friend, follow him, and to tell others.

Before you fill out this prayer invitation from Jesus to you, pray that God will show you how to follow him in your life. Ask him to show you which friend to pray for to also have a friendship with Jesus.

PRAYER INVITATION

This invitation is for ....
to follow Jesus, to go on adventures with him,
and to be his friend.

I, ..., accept this invitation.

I also invite .... to have a friendship
with Jesus. I pray that they will get to know him too.

DROP YOUR NET!

WOW! Jesus asked the disciples to drop their nets and to follow him! They were fishermen and so this was their livelihood, their passion, and where they had community and friends. Leaving all that to follow Jesus would have been hard.

Do you think it was just the actual nets Jesus wanted them to leave or more than that? They were definitely being asked to step out of their comfort zones!

Have you ever had to leave something you loved behind to start something new and exciting? Maybe you have moved to a new house or started at a new school.

Have you ever had to change something about yourself to have a friendship with Jesus? Like choosing to be kind to people even if they are unkind to you? Or stopping yourself getting angry if something frustrates you? Or perhaps saying thank you to people who care for you?

Let's get creative!

In the net below, draw pictures or write down the things that God has asked you to leave behind or to change in order to follow him.

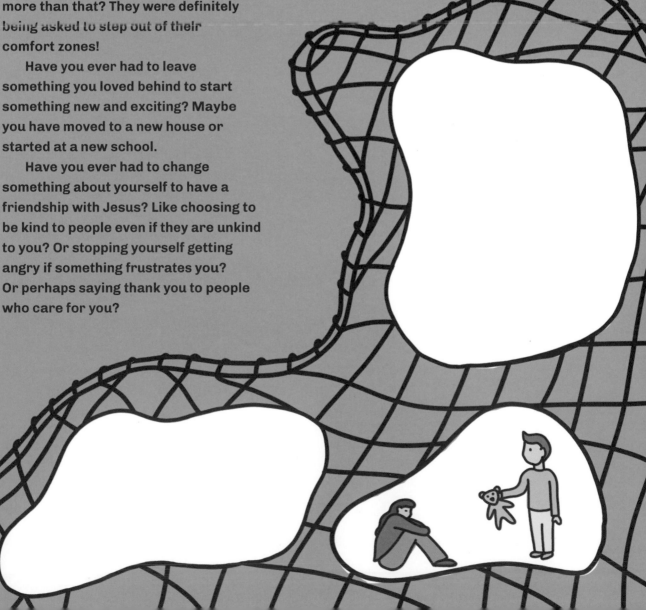

Wow! What a show...

WISH YOU WERE **HERE**

When the disciples followed Jesus, they left all their friends and family behind to go on amazing adventures with him.

I wonder if they even had time to tell their family and friends they were going? Do you think they kept in touch with them while they were away? They must have wanted to tell them all about Jesus and the incredible things they had seen!

Let's act!

It's true, the disciples didn't have the ability to film things back then – they probably would have written a letter! But what if the technology had existed and they were able to send a "video postcard" home?

They would have been able to reassure their family that they were fine, and tell them about Jesus and all the incredible things they were seeing. It would have been pretty cool!

Let's have fun creating a "video postcard" performance.

STEP 1

CREATE A CHARACTER: Using your body, think about how your character will move. Is the way they move fast or slow? Is their voice different to your voice? Is it higher or lower in tone? How does the character use their facial expressions and body language to show their emotions?

STEP 2

BEGINNING AND END: Make a freeze-frame picture (a still pose) of your character that will go at the start and end of your performance.

STEP 3

WRITE YOUR SCRIPT: Start by saying "hello" and end with "goodbye". Write three sentences that your disciple will say in their video postcard. They might mention what Jesus is like, what they've eaten, or a miracle they've seen.

STEP 4

REHEARSE AND PERFORM: Add your freeze-frames to open and close your video postcard. Rehearse until you feel ready to perform what you have created to an audience.

FILL UP THE BOAT

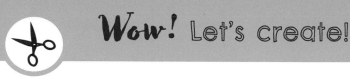

WOW! After Jesus performed his miracle, the disciples caught so many fish! Jesus then called them to be fishers of people.

As friends of Jesus, we are also called to be fishers of people – to pray for our friends that they too will have an amazing friendship with God!

Let's get creative!

Create a "fish garland" to remind you of this incredible miracle and what Jesus asks us to do.

YOU WILL NEED:

colourful paper or card
pens
things to decorate your fish with
   (e.g. sequins and stickers)
string and scissors
a hole punch

STEP 1 Cut multiple fish shapes of different sizes out of the coloured card.

STEP 2 Decorate each fish differently to make them look bright and unique.

STEP 3 On the back of each fish, write the name of a friend who you would like to get to know Jesus.

STEP 4 Punch a hole in one end of each fish shape.

STEP 5 Tie all the fish shapes together so they dangle down.

STEP 6 Hang the fish up to brighten a room. They will remind you of Jesus' miracle and to pray for your friends!

BBQ ON THE BEACH

There is another story in the Bible where Jesus performed a similar miracle (you can find it in John 21:1–14). However, this was after the disciples had known Jesus for a long time!

This time, instead of asking the disciples to follow him he invited them to eat breakfast with him and to just hang out! But this wasn't just any old breakfast – it was a barbecue on the beach!

Isn't it cool how Jesus liked sharing food and spending time with people, especially his close friends? To celebrate and remember how Jesus wants to spend time with us too why don't you have a barbecue (for breakfast – or at another time) with your friends?

Let's get creative!

Ask an adult to help you pack up a small outdoor barbecue or create your own "fire torch" to cook on, then find a place outside to spend time together.

If your friends don't know the story of Jesus and the fishermen, why not tell them about it?

FIRE TORCH:

⚠️ For this activity, you will need adult help, a safe place to light a fire, and a bucket of water to put the fire out.

STEP 1 Find a large log and stand it up on its end.

STEP 2 Create two large cuts, making a cross through the log until you reach 8cm (3in) from the bottom. (For larger logs you will need to make more cuts.)

STEP 3 Fill the gap with dry lint material and cover the top with a few bits of kindling (small pieces of dry wood).

STEP 4 Light the lint and kindling until the middle of the log catches fire.

STEP 5 When the fire is going, use long sticks to toast marshmallows over your fire and have a great time with your friends!

EMOTION EXPLOSION

"We've been fishing for hours and we're so tired!"

"WOW! We've caught so many fish!"

"Who is this Jesus?"

"Should we leave behind what we know and love, to go with him?"

WOW! The disciples must have had so many emotions going through their heads!

What a mix of feelings to have in such a short time! Has there ever been a time when you felt lots of different emotions in a short space of time?

Let's get creative!

Below, fill in the faces with the emotions you think the disciples felt. Can you think of a time when you felt emotions like these?

Riding the Waves!

The story of Jesus calming the storm

MATTHEW 4:35–41

Jesus and his disciples were exhausted after another busy day. So, they got in a boat and started rowing across a lake called the Sea of Galilee. They needed a bit of space to chill.

Jesus was especially tired, so he told his mates he was going to take a break and cosied up with a pillow among the fishing nets for a nap.

Out on the lake, the weather can change very quickly. Winds can become very fierce and stormy in just a few seconds, which was exactly what Jesus and his disciples were about to see.

The breeze became a howling wind and the heavens opened with lightning and hail! Those type of conditions are very scary when you are on open water.

The disciples put on their raincoats. They hoped the storm would pass but it only got worse – and so did their fear. Could this be their last day on earth?

They shook Jesus awake, who told them not to worry! Didn't they trust that they would be alright with him in the boat to protect them?

Jesus got up, lifted his hands over the water, and said, "Be still!" The wind settled down and the storm stopped dead.

This was a mind-blowing moment for Jesus' mates. They realized Jesus' awesome power!

Wow! What a story! What a miracle!

WANT TO READ MORE?
Why not dive into the story by reading it in your Bible in **MATTHEW 4:35–41?**

OR you could start your creative adventure exploring this amazing story about Jesus right away!

I KNOW YOU'RE THERE!

When the disciples were in the middle of the storm, they began to panic! They were scared of what was around them – and terrified they would die.

However, Jesus was in the boat with them the whole time. He wouldn't let them come to any harm.

When Jesus woke up, he asked them why they didn't trust him even though they knew he was there with them.

Have you ever felt like this? It can feel hard to remember God is there when it feels like there is "a storm" in our lives. You may be scared about something that is happening in the news, or perhaps you are worried about a friend who is sick. Maybe you are anxious about a problem at school or you might be scared of moving to a new area.

Let's get creative!

Look at the prayer poem below.

Can you finish the end of each sentence with something about your own life? When you have filled in the lines, read the prayer poem out loud. Use this to help you remember that God is always there with you in everything.

When I'm sad because ....
  I know you're there.

When I'm worried about ....
  I know you're there.

When I'm overwhelmed by ....
  I know you're there.

At the start of the day, at the end of the day,
  And all the way through,
  I know you're there.
  I know you're there.
  I know you're there.

Wow! Time to pause...

BE STILL

Have you ever heard the phrase, "A storm in a teacup"? It's a funny phrase, isn't it? It means someone is very angry or feeling strong emotions about something that isn't a big deal to other people.

The thing is, no matter how big or small our worries or feelings are to other people, to God they always matter. There is no "storm in a teacup" with him! He always cares about what we care about.

Just like the story of Jesus telling the storm to be still, he tells the "storms" in our life to "be still" too. Things may not change around us, but he can bring us peace and help us not to be so afraid!

Let's get creative!

It's time to create your own work of art with just some tea, coffee, paper, and pens. Before you know it, you will have an amazing masterpiece to remind you that God tells our worries to "be still" so that we can feel his peace.

STEP 1 Dampen your paper and use the tea and coffee to make water marks on your page to create the effect of moving water. The wetter the paper, the more the tea and coffee will be able to move on the page.

STEP 2 Create different shades of the stains by using more or less tea and coffee. This will create the effect of strong waves on the page.

STEP 3 Once you are happy with the art you have created, leave it to dry.

STEP 4 Now the paper is completely dry, use your pen to write on top of the wave shapes, "BE STILL".

STEP 5 Place your picture somewhere you can see it. Ask God to be with you and bring peace in the middle of your own storms.

YOU WILL NEED:

tea bags
coffee granules
a bold pen
paper
water

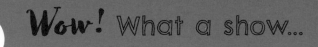

HEAVE! HO!

WOW! There is so much drama in this story about Jesus calming the storm!

Just like every good tale, there is a dramatic build-up as the storm gets wilder and wilder, and the disciples start to fear for their lives.

There is the brilliant climax as the storm waves crash over the side of the boat and Jesus wakes up just in time!

Then the story finishes with an uplifting ending as the disciples can't help but worship Jesus!

Let's act!

This story has the plot line every actor dreams of. So, here's your chance to do some acting, take the starring role, and turn the story into a gripping performance!

STEP 1

CREATE YOUR SET: First create a boat. Ask an adult what you're able to use and where it's safe to make your set. You could use an upside down table or cushions shaped like a boat.

STEP 2

CREATE YOUR ROLE: Decide which character from the story you will play. Can you use your facial expressions and body language to show the character's emotions throughout the scene?

STEP 3

CHOOSE YOUR SOUNDTRACK: Pick an exciting piece of music that expresses the drama of the storm.

STEP 4

CREATE YOUR STORY ARK: A story ark is how the beginning, middle, and end of a story flow together. Use the storm growing in strength and the climax of Jesus waking up as part of the story ark for your scene.

STEP 5

MIME OR DIALOGUE: Decide whether you would like your characters to speak or mime throughout your scene, with the music as a soundtrack.

STEP 6

REHEARSE: Practise your scene and then find an audience to watch your performance!

LIGHTS! CAMERA! ACTION!

In films, directors sometimes use slow motion to make a scene really tense.

If a director was making a film about the story of Jesus calming the storm, do you think they would use slow motion to make the storm scene dramatic?

Get ready to create your own stop-motion movie!

Let's get creative!

A fun way of creating your own slow-motion scene from the story is to create a stop-motion video. By adding a series of photographs together, it can look like a moving picture but in slow motion.

STEP 1 Using items in your house (such as a washing-up bowl filled with water, a tub for a boat, and any small figures you may have), create a small set that you can move and photograph to tell the story.

STEP 2 Create a "shot list" for your story. This is where you write a list of all the photographs you want to take to make sure you capture the whole story. For stop motion to work really well, the smaller the changes between each photo, the better!

STEP 3 Set up your first "shot". In the correct order, slightly moving the objects for each picture, begin to take your photos.

STEP 4 Once you have taken your photos, you can either edit them together to make a stop-motion film or you can flick quickly through your photos to see the effect of the pictures moving!

TOP TIPS:
• Keep your camera on something like a pile of books to stop it from moving in between shots.
• Make very small changes to the set and figures between shots. When you add all the photos together, it gives a brilliant slow-motion effect!

SWOOSH, WOOSH, TWIST, AND TURN

The disciples were so astounded by what Jesus did that they were even a little bit scared. His power was so great that he could calm the storm and the waves!

How do you think you would have felt if you had been there? Do you think you would have been amazed at Jesus'

miracle? Sometimes, when we are overwhelmed with admiration for God, we can't help but worship him and praise him for his great power.

A great way to praise God is by using our bodies to worship him!

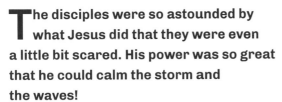

Let's get creative!

In this space, draw the shapes of the waves, twisting, turning, and crashing against the boat. Use shapes that are powerful and have curves as well as straight edges.

Look at the shapes you have drawn. With your whole body, recreate the shapes of the waves in large, powerful movements.

Play a piece of music and use the wave movements as worship to God for how powerful he is.

THE STORM WILL CEASE

Sometimes, it can feel like we are in a storm of our own. Have you ever felt overwhelmed by something that was going on in your life? Have your emotions ever felt so big that you didn't know how to control them? This is totally normal. Life can be overwhelming and difficult at times. However, God wants to bring peace in your heart just like Jesus brought peace to the lake in the story.

Let's get creative!

Let's make a storm jar full of water, glitter, and sequins. When you shake it, the glitter will spiral quickly around the jar. But when the jar is held still, the glitter will begin to settle.

YOU WILL NEED:

a jam jar or a plastic bottle with a lid
glitter and sequins
water

STEP 1 Put about 2 tablespoons of glitter and sequins into the bottom of your jar or bottle.

STEP 2 Fill two-thirds of your jar or bottle with water.

STEP 3 Replace the lid of your bottle or jar.

STEP 4 When things seem too much, you can shake the jar and watch as the water and glitter settle. Be reminded that God brings peace in your storm too.

It will remind you of how Jesus calmed the storm, and of how you can ask him to calm the "storms" in your life too.

Open Up the Ceiling!

The story of Jesus healing the paralyzed man

MARK 2:1–12

A few men had heard that Jesus was in town and was speaking in a house close by.

Lots of people were excited about this and were going to see Jesus. However, for these men in particular, it was extra-important to meet him.

You see, their mate was not very well. He was paralyzed, which meant that he couldn't move his body at all. The men were carrying him on a woven mat toward the house where Jesus was speaking. They knew that if they managed to get their mate close to Jesus, then he could heal him so he could walk again! This encounter could be life-changing!

Imagine how frustrated the men were when they turned up at the house and couldn't get in! It was rammed full of people.

They tried squeezing their mate through the front door, but no luck! They tried squeezing him through the back door, but no luck! They even tried every window they could find, but no luck!

Then the men came up with a clever plan. "We'll make a hole in the roof and lower him down!"

The friends got to work and began to chisel a hole through the roof of the building. It got bigger and bigger until they could see right into the packed house. Then they started to lower their mate down (good job he wasn't scared of heights), and they rested him right at Jesus' feet.

The room was silent as Jesus looked up to see the friends grinning down at him. Jesus beamed back and looked at the guy lying at his feet. "Your friends' faith has healed you. Get up and walk!"

The man bent one leg. Then he bent the other leg. He lifted himself up, standing tall in front of Jesus and the whole crowd!

Smiling back at Jesus, the man danced out of that building. He was changed forever after an encounter with Jesus!

Wow! What a story! What a miracle!

WANT TO READ MORE?
Why not dive into the story by reading it in your Bible in
MARK 2:1–12?

OR you could start your creative adventure exploring this amazing story about Jesus right away!

Wow! Hello God...

A POT FOR PRAYERS

Friendship is an amazing thing! Friends get to laugh together, make memories together, and be there for each other through hard times.

When our friends share their worries or problems with us and we are able to tell them that we are praying for them, it is even more special. Especially when we believe that Jesus can really help them in their struggle.

Let's get creative!

In the story about the paralyzed man, Jesus saw the faith of the man's friends and healed him! Their faith in Jesus really changed things – and our prayers for our friends can too.

Why not make a little prayer jar to prompt you to pray for your friends? Each day, you could pick out a different friend's name and pray for them!

YOU WILL NEED:

a jar to decorate
paint pens for glass,
  or other decorations
lolly sticks
coloured pens

STEP 1 Decorate your jar using the pens for glass, or other decorations. Make it colourful and eye-catching!

STEP 2 Decorate each stick with a different friend's name, beautiful colours, and shapes.

STEP 3 Put the sticks in the jar and pull one out. The name on the stick is the person to pray for! Pray whatever encouraging words come into your head for your friend.

THERE MUST BE ANOTHER WAY!

Did you notice in the story how the friends found it really hard to get into the building to see Jesus? They tried every window and every door – in the end they had to burrow down from the roof! They must have been so determined to see him.

Have you ever had things that stopped you from talking to God? Maybe you were too busy? Perhaps you got distracted as you went to read your Bible? Whatever it is, there is always another chance to meet with Jesus!

Let's get creative!

In each of the doors and windows, draw or write down the things that stop you from chatting with God. As you draw, ask God to help you in your faith to always find a way to meet with him.

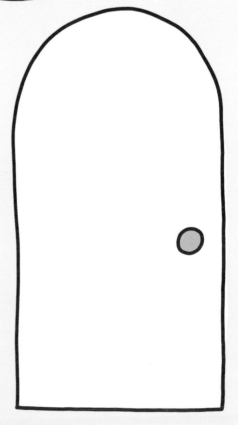

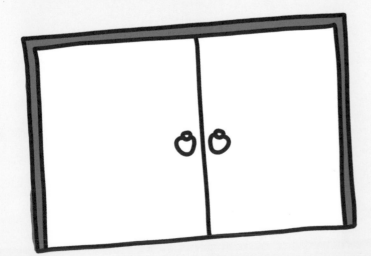

Wow! What a show...

OUR DRAMA THIS WEEK IS...

Jesus was standing in the middle of a crowded room. The noise and bustle of everyone crammed together, just trying to catch a glimpse of him, was frantic. More and more people kept coming through the door and windows, sitting on every available surface. There was no room left: no one else could fit in!

Then a scratching sound began. There was a bash and a bang, and then a chink of light appeared from up above. Dust and dirt began to fall as the hole grew in size. Suddenly, the roof caved in, and peeking down were a few people all looking hopeful and slightly nervous!

They started to shuffle and shift something that the crowd couldn't yet see. What was it – a bed or a mat perhaps? Whatever it was began to get bigger and the crowd realized the people on the roof were lowering it into the room. Something... or someone!

Then the crowd fell silent as a man lying on a mat was gently placed by Jesus' feet.

Let's act!

What a story! What enthusiastic sounds there would have been coming from so many people. This is a story that needs to be told – by you!

It's time to create your own **RADIO DRAMA**. A radio drama is a play that is performed and recorded using only actors' voices. In radio plays, the scene is set by making sound effects of the location and people to create an atmosphere.

STEP 1

SET YOUR SCENE: Create a soundscape to open your drama and create an atmosphere. A soundscape is lots of sounds all layered on top of each other. Using your voices and objects around you, build up sounds to show the atmosphere in the room.

STEP 2

WRITE YOUR SCRIPT: Once you have created a soundscape, have a go at writing a script for the rest of the drama. Before writing your script, think about these questions:

- Do you two want two characters talking to each other or a narration from one person?
- Which characters from the story do you want to write into your drama?
- What is the climax in the middle of the story?
- What atmosphere do you want to create with the sound effects you make?

STEP 3

REHEARSE AND RECORD: Once you have finished your script and sound effects, give your drama a title. Rehearse your script and record it on a phone or laptop. Now, find an audience to listen to your fantastic radio drama!

WOVEN REMINDERS

In the story of the paralyzed man, his friends carried him on a woven mat to see Jesus. That mat must have been really strong, and his friends must have been strong too to carry him! How do you think the man felt when Jesus healed him so he could walk again? He must have been overjoyed by what had happened!

Let's get creative!

Why not make your own woven mats to use as coasters and placemats to remind you of the miracle Jesus performed in this story?

STEP 1 Cut 2cm (¾ in) strips along both pieces of material, leaving a 2cm (¾ in) border on one edge.

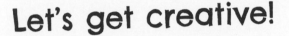

STEP 2 Put both squares of material on top of each other, with the non-cut edges making a right angle.

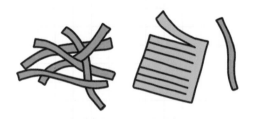

STEP 3 With the top piece of material, weave each 2cm (¾ in) strand of material over and under the pieces of cut fabric on the bottom square.

STEP 4 Repeat until all the material is woven and a square mat is made. Tie two strips together all along the end of the weave in small knots so it does not fray.

TOP TIP: You could attach your material onto a piece of wood or card with glue, making it really secure to use as a coaster or placemat!

DISCO PRAISE PARTY!

Imagine years of not being able to move your body at all. Years of not being able to go for a walk in the park, or even to stand or sit up by yourself.

Now, imagine how the paralyzed man, who had not been able to move his body for years, felt when he was healed by Jesus.

He could move his arms and his legs! He could pick up his own mat and walk out of that building praising Jesus!

Why don't you take time to praise God for your own body and the way it moves? All our bodies move in different ways, outside and inside. From the blood pumping around your body to how you move your fingers and toes, there is always a reason to praise Jesus for our bodies!

So go on, have a disco praise party now! Put on some music and let your body dance and move in whatever way you can. Celebrate the body God has given you and praise him for the wonderful work he has done!

BUT **WHAT IS** FAITH?

In Hebrews 11:1, we read, "Now faith is being sure of what we hope for and certain of what we do not see." The word "faith" can be so confusing, and can mean different things to different people.

What is faith? What does faith mean to you? Can we have faith in other things as well as faith in God?

Faith in God

Let's get creative!

Fill in the circles with what faith means to you in each situation. Why not chat with someone as you fill it out and ask them what they think too?

Faith in family and friends

Faith in the world

Laz! Come Out!

The story of Jesus resurrecting Lazarus

JOHN: 11:1-45

It had been a bad few days for Jesus and his friends Mary and Martha. You see, Mary and Martha were sisters, and their brother Lazarus was very poorly.

Laz was Jesus' friend. When he became really ill, Mary asked Jesus to come and heal him.

The trouble was that Jesus didn't turn up in time and Lazarus breathed his last breath.

Martha was devastated and Mary was torn apart. When Jesus arrived, Mary demanded, "Where were you, Jesus? If you'd been here, Lazarus would not have died!"

This was too much for Jesus. His good friend was gone and grief engulfed him. He sat with Mary and wept.

Jesus turned to Mary and asked her, "Didn't I tell you that if you believe, you'd see the glory of God?"

Standing up with urgency, he walked over to Laz's tomb and roared the words, "Lazarus, come out!" Moments later, Lazarus was stumbling out of his tomb. He was wrapped in cloth, gasping and gulping for air!

Lazarus was alive and thriving!

Wow! What a story! What a miracle!

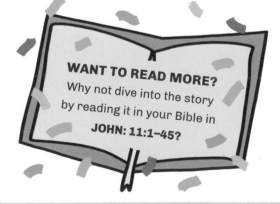

WANT TO READ MORE?
Why not dive into the story by reading it in your Bible in **JOHN: 11:1-45?**

OR you could start your creative adventure exploring this amazing story about Jesus right away!

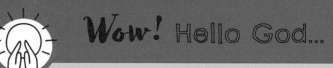
HOPE IN THE WAITING

When you're waiting for something, time seems to go slower!

Waiting for a bus... Waiting for a message... Waiting for a friend to visit.

This was definitely the case for Mary and Martha as they waited for Jesus to arrive when their brother Lazarus was sick. They knew that Jesus could help him, but it seemed as though they had waited too long! Jesus didn't come in time and Lazarus died.

However, Jesus then arrived and performed the most incredible miracle he could. He bought his friend back to life!

When Mary and Martha were waiting for Jesus, it must have been incredibly hard to keep hoping that he could help them. But when Mary saw Jesus, her heart burst with hope in him.

Let's get creative!

Take time to plant a bulb or some seeds, placing the pot somewhere you can see it.

As you wait for the plant to show and grow, pray each day that God will be with you in the waiting.

Pray that God will remind you that when it feels like hope isn't there, he will give you patience and faith to hope in him.

When the plant shows and grows, thank God for the hope he gives to us and our friendship with him.

|| Wow! Time to pause...

JESUS, ARE YOU **THERE?**

Mary trusted her friend Jesus to be there when she most needed him. Lazarus was one of Jesus' friends too. However, when she really needed Jesus' help, Mary felt like he had abandoned her!

Have you ever felt like God wasn't there in a moment when you really needed him? Maybe when something sad happened or when you were worried or scared?

Mary tried to contact Jesus to tell him to hurry. How do you think she was feeling? Frustrated? Angry? Helpless? Hopeful?

Let's get creative!

Write a letter from Mary to Jesus in the space here, without thinking too much about the words. Imagine she is writing this letter just after Lazarus' death, when Jesus was still not with them. What do you think she would have written? Mary and Jesus were good friends and had been for a long time.

Lazarus had risen from the dead! THIS WAS A MIRACLE! Nothing like it had ever happened before. Everyone who saw this happen couldn't stop talking about it.

Lazarus had been dead for three days, but Jesus came and called him out of the tomb. There he was. Alive!

This was BIG NEWS!

BREAKING NEWS!

Let's act!

What a story! Follow the steps below to create a BREAKING NEWS report!

STEP 1

FIND YOUR PROPS: Get a wooden spoon to use as a microphone, and a clipboard or notebook to read the "breaking news" from.

STEP 2

CREATE YOUR CHARACTER: You will be playing the role of a news presenter. Decide how you want your character to sound when presenting the news. Will they be doing their job professionally, or showing amazement too?

STEP 3

CREATE YOUR NEWS REPORT: Decide what you want to say in your report. Will it be just the facts, or will you say how you feel about this extraordinary thing that has happened?

STEP 4

REHEARSE AND PERFORM: Practise your piece until it is ready to perform. Gather an audience and tell them about this incredible breaking news!

TOP TIP: If there are other people taking part, they could play the role of witnesses. You could ask them questions about what exactly they saw as they describe this astonishing event.

Wow! Let's create!

FROM DARKNESS TO LIGHT!

Imagine what it must have felt like for Lazarus scrambling from the darkness of the tomb into the bright light of day...
What a journey of HOPE! A journey toward LIGHT! A journey to JESUS!

Let's get creative!

Create your own "dark to light" obstacle course as a reminder that Jesus calls us out of the darkness and into the light.

STEP 1 Gather chairs, cushions, and thick duvets from around your house. Use these at the start of the obstacle course to create pitch-black tunnels and paths.

STEP 2 Further along in the obstacle course, use thinner materials to crawl under such as sheets and scarves. These will let the light shine through them more and more as you move toward the end of the course.

STEP 3 Once you have created your obstacle course, ask people to move through it. Ask them what it felt like moving from pitch darkness toward bright light!

TOP TIP: Use lamps and torches toward the end of your obstacle course to create even more LIGHT!

APPRECIATION POST!

Have you noticed how we sometimes miss the opportunity to tell people how much we appreciate them or how amazing we think they are? We often don't realize these things until someone has passed away, moved away, or even just changed class or school. It's when we don't see someone as much as before that we really wish we could tell them how much we love them and how great they are!

Mary and Martha were able to see their brother Lazarus again after realizing how much they missed him. Do you think they told him how much they loved him?

What if you didn't wait until someone was not there to give them kind compliments? What if you were to tell your friends and family how much you appreciated them every day? What if you celebrated who they are, and all the things you think are great about them, whenever you spent time with them?

Do you think telling your friends these things would make them feel differently? It would probably give them confidence and make them feel really appreciated and loved!

Let's get creative!

Why not send some appreciation post?

In the space here, draw a picture of a friend who you have not seen for a while. Around your picture, write all the positive thoughts you have about them – what makes them a good friend, what you admire about them, what they do that makes you laugh, and why you are thankful that they are your friend.

Once you have all these positive thoughts, it's time to tell your friend! Write down all your words of encouragement in a letter or a card and post it to your friend as a surprise. It will make them feel loved and appreciated! If you want to spread a little more love, maybe you could send more appreciation post to other friends too?

Wow! Can we chat?

I MISS YOU

When Jesus arrived at the scene of Lazarus' tomb, I wonder if he was expecting to see what he found? Lazarus was one of his closest friends and Jesus arrived to discover he was dead.

Mary and Martha had lost their brother and many people in the village had lost a close friend. What emotions do you think they were feeling?

Grief is a difficult emotion. It is very sad when someone dies, and it can leave us feeling empty and really missing them.

However, often when someone passes away, we are also left with so many amazing memories of who they were and the wonderful times we had with them.

Let's get creative!

With an adult, think about someone or something you have lost or had to leave behind. It may be a person or a pet, or it could be a place (if you moved to a new house, for example).

Light a candle. Then remember and share some wonderful memories you have of that person, pet, or place.

I'm Coming for Tea!

The story of Jesus meeting Zacchaeus

JERICHO

LUKE 19:1–10

People were making a habit of gathering when they heard that Jesus was in town. He'd become a bit of a celebrity and so the people of Jericho weren't going to miss him walking through their town for all the sandals in Bethlehem!

One guy called Zacchaeus was a lot shorter than most people. His little legs hadn't carried him fast enough to get a front-row seat, so he was stuck at the back of the crowd with a terrible view!

He wanted to see Jesus as much as the next person. But Zac was a little different from other people. He took money from people for a living, making sure they gave him what they owed to their town and then taking the profits for himself. Basically, he was as greedy as a slug in a lettuce patch!

Zac hatched a genius plan to climb to the top of a tree to get the best view of Jesus strolling by. When Jesus made his big entrance, he stopped on the road, looked up at the trees, and stared straight at Zacchaeus!

"Hey Zac, come down from that tree! Want to make me a cuppa and have a good catch up?"

The crowd couldn't believe that Jesus wanted to spend time with Zac – but that was a turning point in his story.

After that meeting between Jesus and Zac behind closed doors, something happened that made everyone's lives a little better. Zacchaeus was a changed man!

He gave people their money back plus a little bit more, and he made a point of being as kind to people as he possibly could. I guess that is what a cuppa with Jesus is bound to do to you!

Wow! What a story! What a miracle!

WANT TO READ MORE?
Why not dive into the story by reading it in your Bible in
LUKE 19:1–10?

OR you could start your creative adventure exploring this amazing story about Jesus right away!

SPOT THE DIFFERENCE

Wasn't it cool how after Zacchaeus spent time with Jesus, he was a completely different person? He changed the way he treated people, how he spoke to them, and how he dealt with the money he had been given.

Have a look at the two pictures of Zacchaeus below. Can you spot the differences between them that show how he was before he met Jesus, and how he was after he met Jesus?

Let's get creative!

Why don't you draw your own "spot the difference"? Draw a picture of yourself and ask God to show you the ways in which you could change to be more like Jesus. Maybe it's by being kind to people? Or by helping others if they need a hand?

CAN YOU SPOT THE DIFFERENCE?

DIFFERENCES: The sun is out, a bird is flying around, two cups of tea, not holding on to the bag of money, Zacchaeus is happy!

Draw a second picture of yourself after you've "spent time with God".
Pray that he will help you to spend more time talking to him. Ask him to
teach how you can be kind and care for other people in your life.

BEHIND CLOSED DOORS

What do you think went on behind those closed doors when Jesus and Zacchaeus spent time together? What do you think was said? Wouldn't you love to know? It must have been quite something if it changed Zacchaeus so much.

Do you ever wonder what Jesus wants to say to you behind closed doors? It would be something personal between you and him, that no one else can hear.

Let's get creative!

Create your own "ponder and pause, pop outdoors" to help you reflect on what God may be wanting to say to you in private.

YOU WILL NEED:

2 pieces of card
scissors
tape
coloured pencils
pens

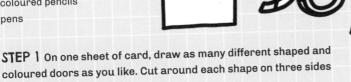

STEP 1 On one sheet of card, draw as many different shaped and coloured doors as you like. Cut around each shape on three sides to make it open like a door.

STEP 2 Tape the blank piece of card to the back of the first piece of card around the edges to create an advent calendar effect.

STEP 3 Take some time to stop and listen to God. Find out what he wants to say to you.

STEP 4 Behind each door flap, write down a word or a sentence that you think God is saying to you.

STEP 5 When you feel like you need a little bit of encouragement, open up a door and read one of the positive messages from God!

TOP TIP:
If you are unsure of what to write behind the doors, you could find some verses in the Bible where we are told what God thinks of us and write one behind each door. For example, "You are loved!" or "You are God's masterpiece!"

TEA WITH ME AT THREE!

What a wonderful afternoon tea Zacchaeus would have laid on for Jesus! The man who everyone was talking about wanted to spend time with HIM! Greedy and unkind Zacchaeus! No one could believe it.

Even Zacchaeus struggled to believe it. However, he would throw the best tea party ever to really impress Jesus with how important and rich he was.

The thing is, this tea party didn't quite turn out the way that Zacchaeus thought it would.

Let's act!

Create a scene telling the story of Jesus meeting Zacchaeus.

STEP 1

BUILD A SET: Find some objects around your house to create a set of Zacchaeus' dining room. Make your set look very posh to show how wealthy Zacchaeus is.

STEP 2

CREATE YOUR CHARACTER: You will play the role of Zacchaeus. Others with you can play the roles of Jesus and the food servers. Decide how your character walks, talks, and moves. Does this change at all during the scene?

STEP 3

WORK OUT YOUR MIME: Using mime, you will create "Zacchaeus' tea party with Jesus". How will you show how Zacchaeus' personality changes as he spends time with Jesus? You could exaggerate facial expressions and body language. You could also use music as a soundtrack.

STEP 4

SLOW-MOTION CLIMAX: Decide at which point in your scene the "change climax" will come – the moment when Jesus' words to Zacchaeus cause him change his ways for the better. Make this part of the scene "slow-motion", to clearly pinpoint a moment of change in Zacchaeus.

STEP 5

REHEARSE AND PERFORM: Practise your scene until you are confident with it. Find people to be your audience and perform the scene to them!

Wow! Let's create!

>> 45

A TREE TO SEE JESUS

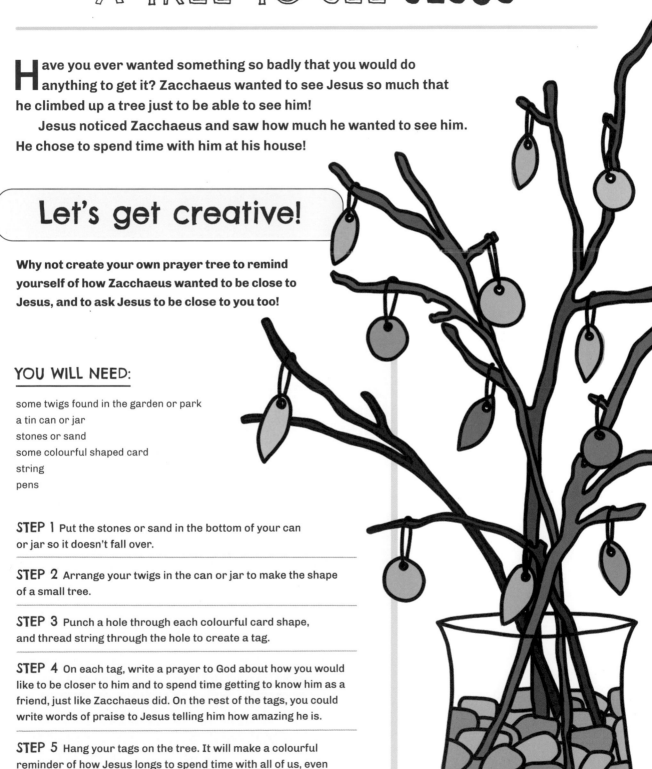

Have you ever wanted something so badly that you would do anything to get it? Zacchaeus wanted to see Jesus so much that he climbed up a tree just to be able to see him!

Jesus noticed Zacchaeus and saw how much he wanted to see him. He chose to spend time with him at his house!

Let's get creative!

Why not create your own prayer tree to remind yourself of how Zacchaeus wanted to be close to Jesus, and to ask Jesus to be close to you too!

YOU WILL NEED:

some twigs found in the garden or park
a tin can or jar
stones or sand
some colourful shaped card
string
pens

STEP 1 Put the stones or sand in the bottom of your can or jar so it doesn't fall over.

STEP 2 Arrange your twigs in the can or jar to make the shape of a small tree.

STEP 3 Punch a hole through each colourful card shape, and thread string through the hole to create a tag.

STEP 4 On each tag, write a prayer to God about how you would like to be closer to him and to spend time getting to know him as a friend, just like Zacchaeus did. On the rest of the tags, you could write words of praise to Jesus telling him how amazing he is.

STEP 5 Hang your tags on the tree. It will make a colourful reminder of how Jesus longs to spend time with all of us, even those people who don't have many friends.

Wow! That's cool!

A PIECE OF CAKE!

It's so cool in the story when Zacchaeus was so changed by Jesus that he gave everyone their money back! Not just some of it, but more money than people gave him in the first place! Zacchaeus was even overjoyed to be giving money away.

God loves it when he sees us being generous and cheerful as we give to other people. Can you think of a time when you gave something to someone that made you really happy? Maybe they were really delighted when you gave it to them, and that made you pleased too?

Why not create something that you can cheerfully give away to someone? It could be a tasty bag of biscuits or a colourful drawing. Or it could be a piece of delicious homemade cake!

Whatever it is you choose to create, cheerfully give it away to someone. It should brighten up their day and make them feel cheerful too!

Let's get creative!

Draw or write below a plan of what you're going to make to cheerfully give to someone else!

SPEAKING WITH YOUR BODY

Quite often, when we feel something on the inside it will show in our body language on the outside. Different emotions and feelings can make us look different in the way we stand or walk.

Let's act!

Have you ever noticed yourself standing in a different way when something made you feel cross, or when you felt excited?

Can you change the way you move your body to show these different emotions?

Do you think Zacchaeus looked different after he spent time with Jesus compared with how he looked before?

Can you use your body to show how Zacchaeus moved around before meeting Jesus? Can you use your body to show how Zacchaeus moved around after spending time with Jesus?

Nervous

Sad

Angry

Excited

Happy

Shy

How does your body language change? Which emotions do you think are more positive, and why?

WOW!

What an epic journey we've had together, Creative Explorer!

Now you know a few of the awesome stories about Jesus, why not tell your friends about how amazing he is and all the cool things he did?

You could even show them some of the things you have created along the way.

The great thing is you can use all of these creative ideas again and again! They can be used on your own, in small groups, or in big groups.

The important thing is to never stop exploring, to never stop discovering new things, and of course to never stop having fun being creative!

Hope to see you again, Creative Explorer!

For more creative resources visit www.nimbuscollective.org

Look Out for

WOW! Christmas
ISBN 978 1 7812 8424 7